MW01626038

TEN DAYS IN HAVANA

TEN DAYS IN HAVANA

David M. Spear

DAVID M. SPEAR

For Kathy!

GNOMON PRESS

Best wishes always!

ISBN 978-0-917788-81-9

LIBRARY OF CONGRESS CONTROL NUMBER: 2013948111

PRINTED AND BOUND IN CHINA

Published by Gnomon Press
P.O. Box 475
Frankfort, KY
40602-0475

FOREWORD

How can we experience the energy of someone else's life? The eyes tell us. The language of the face precedes the spoken word—both in pre-history and today when we see a friend walk into the room.

To photographer David Mayo Spear, of Madison, North Carolina, the human face has become the most important subject of his search. As he points out, startlingly, "Look at it the other way: What if you lost your face? You were still you, but you didn't have a face. How would you enact or show the greatest part of your thoughts and feelings to others?"

His new collection, *Ten Days in Havana,* is the running account of David Spear's search for the strongest, most vital, characteristic, and energetic subjects—and faces particular to Cuba. For Spear, the text, like the photograph, is an anti-mystery device, and thus he experiments with text and story to show the nature of Cuba—the humor and resourcefulness, the resilience and the sadness of Havana.

His camera's eye interprets on behalf of the viewer, making social commentary, yes, but does so in a way that can reveal an individual life as a part for the whole. That whole will be an idea for someone else to make about Cuba—their generalization from individual life to lives to a summary statement about an entire culture. Not David's—his search happens in the moment. And that, as we see here, is plenty!

His attraction to photographing the human face is visceral. He feels a primal pull preceding rationality that draws him to certain faces that have for him a "true eye." At that moment there's a power-transfer going on. Does this eye tell its counterpart —the photographer's eye—something honest, frank, hostile or fearful? Is the authentic inner life caught unsuspecting? Is this salient part of the mystery there, in the true eye, in the strongest face, possibly the shadow of death in the liveliest of all?

Spear's best risk-taking adventure occurs when he couples it with making art. For him, the most profound adventure of travel is going in cold and seeing whether he can make something out of very little in the way of tools—just a camera-phone, legs, eyes, and bodily energy. His choice of using an iPhone as project camera, though, is not totally the result of his acting on a daring do-or-die gesture to push back any boundaries of photography.

The truth is that in September, 2011, Spear broke his back, making it difficult for him to carry his heavy Canon EOS 5D on this trip. It was a huge gamble to depend on an iPhone for ten days with no back-up camera or Apple Store nearby. That gamble may, in the end, have been just the odd necessity that gave Spear a better ability than on two previous trips to Cuba to find the most representative yet most energy-radiant.

Midway through Spear's adventure his iPhone quit. Always resourceful, like his Cuban counterparts, he found an Italian tourist on the street who happened to have an iPhone. In quick order she closed the too-many files he had open, and bingo!—the iPhone camera was fully alive again.

Most of the photographs in the following pages were made with his iPhone. I caution viewers not to distract themselves from directly experiencing the life on these pages by trying to tell which ones!

The street is David's workplace where he searches for strong, true faces to represent

Cuba today. It's also the locus of his brave pleasure in seeing and probing the surface flesh—decorated diversely with lipstick or tattoos or freckles or wrinkles—of the living skull for meaning, for how things are related in time, place, and intention.

Linda Whitney Hobson
Durham, North Carolina
February 22, 2013

TEN DAYS IN HAVANA

1. Aida Cifuentes

SPORTS

2. Bazoca / Mosquito Fogger

Picadillo
PERISHABLE-KEEP FROZEN
PARA
PERISHABLE-KEEP FROZEN

3. Ismael

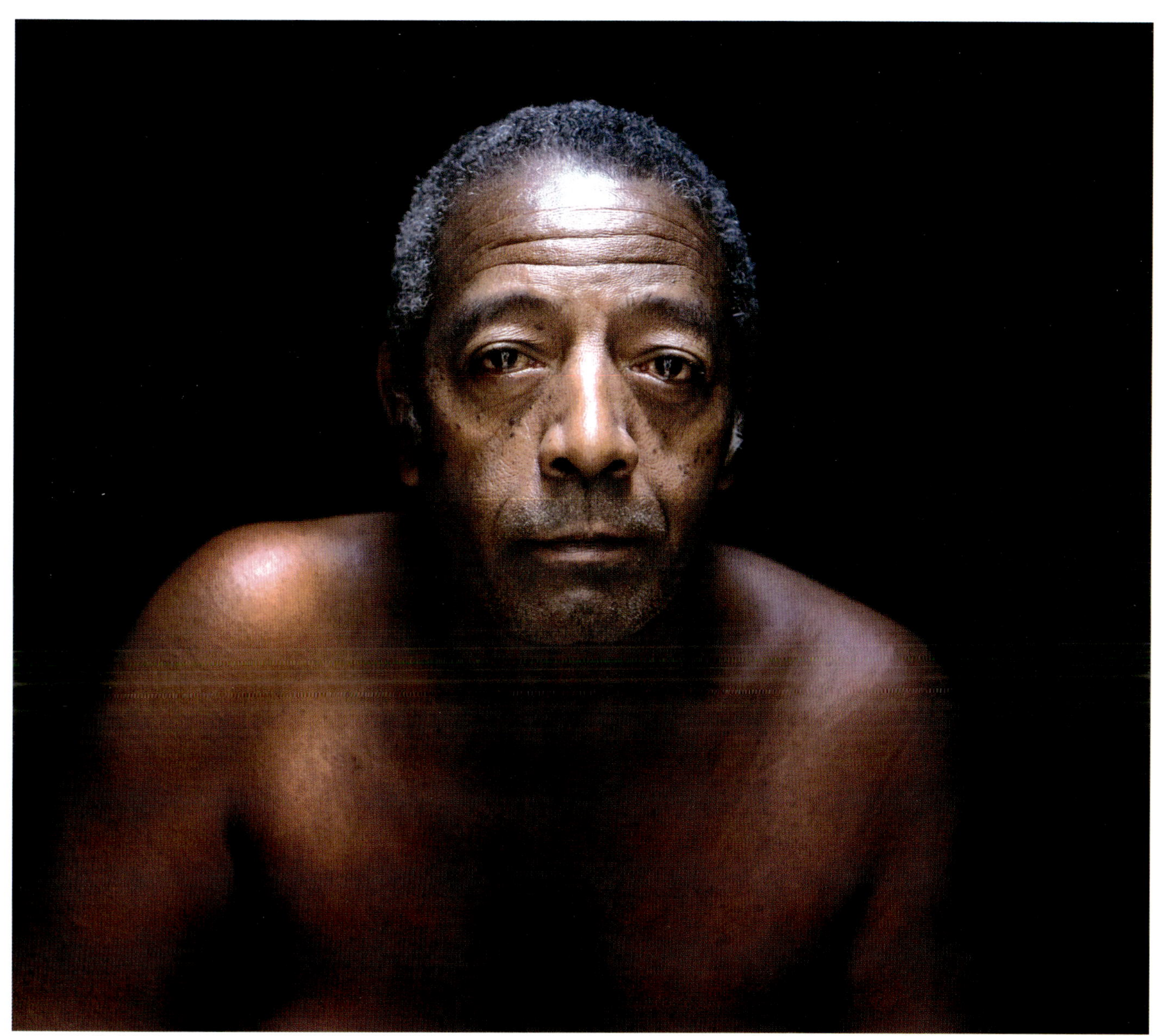

4. Fumigation, Calle San Miguel

HDM 302

5. Carlos y Maria

6. Miguel

7. Leyisett

8. Victor

9. Yanalca

10. Guerra en el Mercado / Guerra in a Market

ALMACÉN
SAN FRANCISCO
San Francisco Authentic
01
AM. AMERICAN BOY

11. Maela

12. Geobar

Leche Entera en polvo

13. Julio

14. Yanire y Estelle

15. Bertha y Ealian

16. Los Pasajeros / The Passengers

17. Domo de Poder para la Memoria /
Power Domes to Improve Memory

18. En la Malecón / At the Seawall

19. Sulema

20. Trabajadores de Azulejo / Tile Workers

21. Metros para los Apartamentos / Apartment Electricity Meters

22. Calle San Raphael

23. Luceda

24. Los Ojos / The Eyes

25. Kireisi

26. Armena

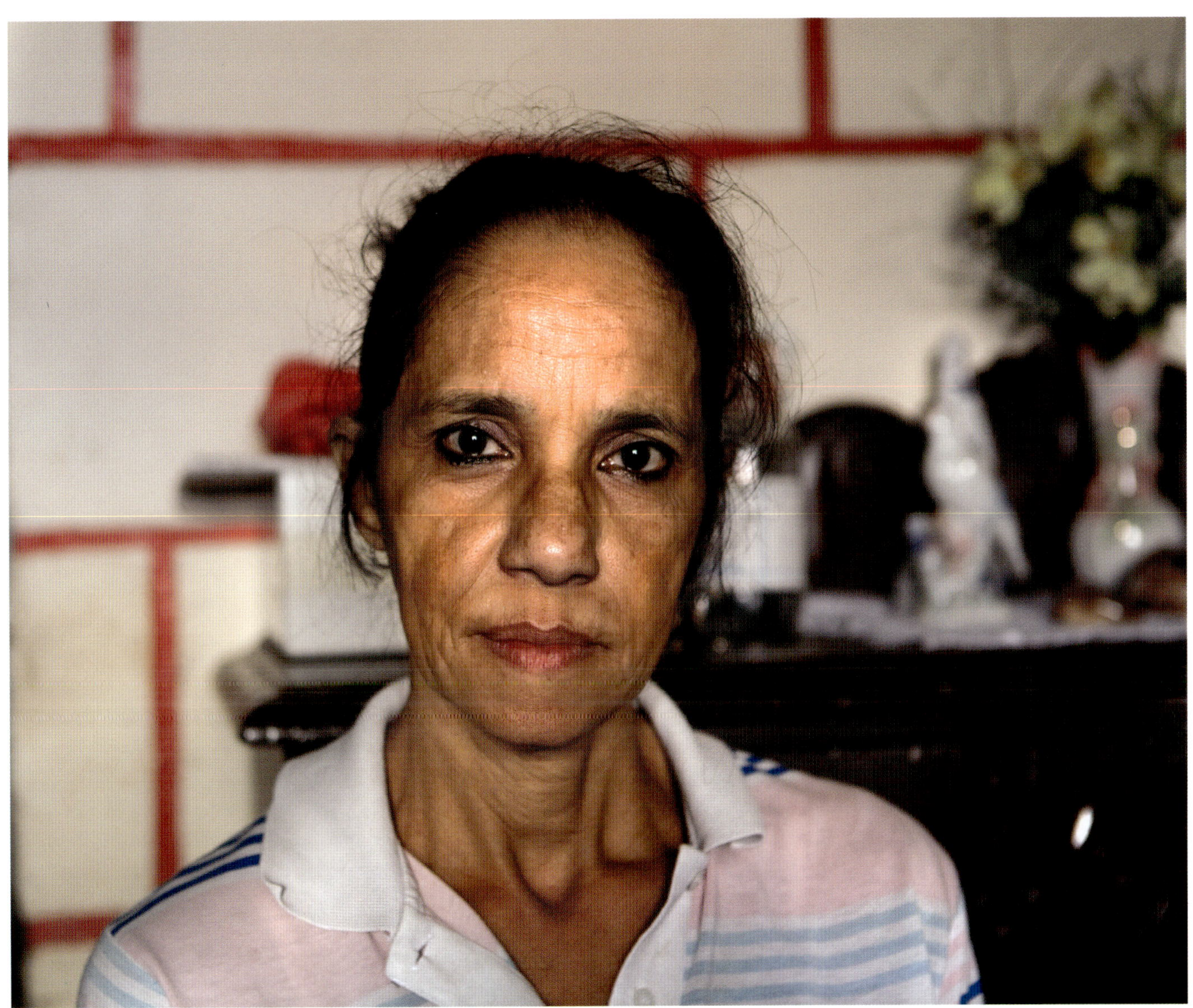

27. Leodanis

28. Reparando los Frenos / Repairing Brakes

29. El Centro Havana

30. Luis Phillipe

31. Aplastado Latas / Flattened Cans

32. Eduardo

MÜNCHEN

33. Juan Carlos y su Hermano Reparando una Bomba /
Juan Carlos and his Brother Repairing a Pump

34. Rolando

TOOL
SET

35. Sonja

36. Tienda de Servicios / Repair Shop

37. Fiesta en Miramar / Party in Miramar

CIEGO

38. Calle Neptune

39. Dominoes en la Calle / Dominoes Played in the Street

Reggetón y Rap

40. Norma Comiendo su Hijo / Norma Nursing her Son

41. En Frente de la Capitolio / Baseball in Front of the Capitol

FSU
12

42. Secando Manteles / Drying Tablecloths

TEN DAYS IN HAVANA

I.

Banu had told me to calm down. "But I need guidance," I told her. I'd been to Cuba twice before and afterward I was not moved by the work I'd done there.

"Can you help me change what I've been doing? I need to get better results, Banu." I had met Banu through the North Carolina Arts Council in Raleigh, where she works as Director of Arts in Education. She is a beautiful, intuitive native Venezuelan. I figured if anyone could help me break into the Latino world, it would be her. "Why don't you try just being still, David. Let Cuba come to you," she suggested. Calming words. Yes, she had tapped into my aggressive, American-born nature. But maybe I could go to Cuba, walk or sit in a relaxed way, and let the people and the photographs come to me. Watch and absorb, be still enough a good bit of the time.

The idea was appealing. Sure, I could move around, but I would walk slowly and engage with people. Still recovering from a broken back I'd suffered in 2011, I knew this would help slow me down.

I was curious to see what Castro had made of Cuba, and I had to be less driven in order to satisfy my curiosity more deeply, more authentically than I had during the two previous trips. I had looked too hard back then—and missed it. As a traveler, I was also looking for a good story. Good stories are hard to find these days. The new generation is so obsessed with the latest techno gadget, they seem to have forgotten the art of telling a good story.

I wanted to understand the essence of the country if that was possible. I decided there was no better place to stay than Havana, the capital. I had worked in Mexico off and on for five years producing the book *Visible Spirits* (Gnomon Press, 2006). I knew that Cuba would be different. No ancient Mayan or Aztec history, no high mountain deserts, no wordless, cryptic, mystical Indian rituals.

How could I authentically characterize Cuba, a less profound and inward-turning culture, with my camera? I might not be able to. Mexico was authentically dramatic in its character and struggles and therefore practically took its own photographs with the assistance of my camera. Cuba was different, a compelling political anomaly banging up against the southern coast of the largest capitalist country in the world; that location made Cuba still defiant, on guard, still socialist, still reproachful, yet still functioning in its isolation––and thus strong of spirit.

Yet a fear of going to Cuba had always been with me, too. My fear was not of Cubans themselves but of FBI agents waiting to grab me in Cancun, Mexico, then rendition me to some remote middle-eastern country and slap me in a cell to be fed crackers and water until I confessed my sin. Since I'd grown up during World War II and the Korean War, I had vivid memories of the Cuban Missile Crisis in October, 1962. So if I traveled to Cuba, I'd be treated like some loathsome traitor to my country, and I imagined pleading with agents, "I'm an honest taxpaying citizen of the United States."

On the two previous trips I had gone to Cancun, Mexico, picked up a visa and a plane ticket in less than an hour. A short flight later I was in Cuba. But those trips were never comfortable. I had heard stories of FBI agents waiting at the airport in Cancun to seize violators of the United States Embargo that had been put in full force by President John F. Kennedy after the Bay of Pigs fiasco in April, 1961.

A story I read in the newspaper after the September 11, 2001, attack on the World Trade Center twin towers reported that FBI agents were in Cancun checking for Americans debarking planes from Cuba. That was probably true considering the foolish ineptness that allowed the attacks of that day to occur despite the many hints of imminent terrorist actions that popped up on government databases during July and August 2001. The government's extreme crackdown on American travelers was in a natural, knee-jerk response to its extreme indifference to potential dangers in the halcyon summer of 2001—and I feared suffering for it.

On one of my return trips to Mexico, in 2002, all American passengers were told to remain in their seats until everyone had exited the plane in Cancun. Fifteen Americans sat there with worried looks on our faces. 'This is it,' I told myself, with a lump in my throat. 'Damn, David! You've been caught.'

Finally we were allowed to leave the plane. In the terminal I cautiously scanned the crowd for ear-wired FBI agents waiting to pounce. Where were they? I asked the airline agent why we were detained.

"Oh!" she said, "We always let the Mexicans leave the plane first."

The Mexicans are still getting back at the United States for stealing their land in the Border Wars of 1846-48. The United States, in winning the conflict, took a good part of California, Utah, New Mexico, Arizona, Colorado, and Texas. The Mexicans have been steaming about it since.

Then there is my American fear of Castro's socialist government. If I carried a computer, would they think I was a CIA agent and slap me in jail? So no computers on this third trip. Wasn't there an American suspected of being a CIA Agent still in a Cuban jail for entering the island nation with a computer?

On an earlier trip, I had made friends with a Cuban painter and on this 2012 trip he wanted me to bring him a computer. "No dice," I said. "I can't take that risk."

To allay my fears, I decided to apply for a U.S. government work permit. If I could go to Cuba with the full backing of the U.S. government, that would calm me down. I had to be calm and free of fear to do good work in Cuba. So after three years of haggling with the U.S. Treasury Department, I got a license to work there in 2011.

One final obstacle was language. Cuban Spanish is fast. I had lived in Mexico during the 1990s until 2003, and I had to work hard to understand taxi drivers who speak rapid Spanish. Before I left for Cuba, then, I decided to stay in Cancun a few days riding in taxis and talking to drivers. The forced immersion spun my brain like a gyroscope, but after two days of these maddening tutorials, I was ready for Cuba.

II.

I had decided not to make clichéd Cuban photographs on this trip—no battered 1950s cars smoking variously white, blue, and gray through the streets of Havana; no black women with colorful scarves wrapped around their heads and/or fat cigars dangling from their lips; not one poster with political information of the thousands plastered throughout the city; no murals of Ernesto 'Che' Guevara or Fidel or brother Raoul, or Jose Marti, the revolutionary poet/philosopher; no riding open tour buses listening to pidgin-English explications of tourist attractions or buildings; and no bicycle taxis, hard not to do for they seem to swarm in Havana like mosquitoes at night. Definitely no gravestones or memorials, and absolutely no photographs of prostitutes this trip. I did, however, make several photographs of unusual buildings.

My first trip to Cuba I had stayed at the Hotel Riviera, built in 1955 by Mafioso Meyer Lansky. He'd filled the enormous lobby with slot machines which Castro had tossed into the sea when he took control of Cuba in 1959. Rooms were large, painted garish pastel colors with monstrous lamps crested with shades the size of barrels. I walked the seawall [the Malecon] to Havana Viejo that first day and was approached by no fewer than a dozen women in an hour who wanted to know if I'd like a woman. I said no diplomatically, expecting an angry response. They were polite, however; "OK, maybe later," they'd say with a smile.

Later that day I decided I should attempt to make photographs of these women to show that Castro had not cleaned up the moral problems of his great city. I told the next woman who asked,"I am interested in a photograph of you."

She smiled and said, "We go to my house."

Soon enough we were there and went down a narrow dark hall into a back room. She closed the door and took off her dress, standing there in bra and panties. She began to dance and I made photographs.

Like a twister out of nowhere two women sailed onto my back, as well as the dancer pinning me to the floor, hands grabbing for my wallet. I'll never forget my first thought as I lay there on that cold tile floor: 'If my mother could only see me now!' An adrenalin burst hit me then and I came off the floor with my tripod swinging, shook the three off me, kicked the door banging it open and scaring myself, and left. I could hear them laughing as I hurried up the street. That was a good first lesson for me: Never go alone with a prostitute into a house.

I decided not to lounge in the garden at the Hotel Nacional to make photographs of the sea and the various garden statues. I did take a look at a surprising collection of photographs of bygone days when movie stars of the 40s and 50s made Havana their playground: Rita Hayworth, Gary Cooper, Clark Gable, Nat King Cole and more. A young Gabriel Garcia Marquez was there, too. And all by himself above a 50s jukebox hung a photograph of Sean Penn in his younger days, with a thin black strip of hair above his upper lip. His dark hair was long and tossed upward, Penn appearing to be playing the part of a subversive, perhaps a revolutionary. But no photographs of Hemingway were in the collection, and I wondered why.

In the hotel Havana Libre, where Castro set up his provisional government headquarters shortly after the revolution in 1959, hang photographs of troops lounging about with machine guns and rifles on the elegant furniture in the lobby.

On the same wall is a photograph of Jane Fonda and Ted Turner. Ubiquitous Jane wears a black dress; a string of large pearls hang down to her navel. I have to say, Jane, you do get around. And there all alone is a portrait of a young Matt Damon.

I would also, I told myself, avoid any photograph that had the trumped-up, chemical slickness of a tourist brochure. No dancing cabaret girls wearing multicolored cha-cha-cha outfits, and least of all no shots of the bronze statue of Ernest Hemingway at the end of the bar in La Floridita, where he hung out with his macho friends, drank, talked loudly.

III.

My mission this trip was to go into the poorest part of the city, then find a place to live and work. From there, I'd photograph the spirit, the resourcefulness, and the real day-to-day lives of the people living in Havana.

I wanted photographs of people who lived and worked in the shops. Could such photographs show what real life is like in Cuba—not the stereotypical tourist shots Americans are used to seeing, images that may mask valuable truths we need to perceive?

Yet all photographs can be duplicitous. Mine would not be free from that challenge to honest reality and working with photographs of people is always more slippery. A building is a building, but a person is complex with constantly changing moods. You can ruin or diminish a person with a camera or you can "focus" on them, not on yourself, and be generous as you try to find something of their personality to record. That was my challenge. I wanted direct facial portraits that might get at some truth about Cubans. And I wanted those faces to tell me an interesting story.

Havana, then, would be my landscape of discovery––a distilled form of the life today in all of Cuba. As a result, all photographs in this book were made in Havana.

Previous trips to Cuba I took along a Hasselblad and later a digital Canon D5. By now I had used the Hasselblad for almost fifteen years with a twelve-exposure film roll that made me take my time and consider each potential photograph.

As the digital age rolled in, Agfa soon quit making their wonderful, warm silver paper, Portriga. I'd worked with it in the darkroom for seventeen years and was beginning to call myself a printer. But with the silver paper no longer available, I thought *Rats, I'd better convert to digital before it's too late!*

Well down the learning curve with computers and all the other new gadgets, I bought a powerful Apple Computer with Photoshop, a Canon EOS D5, got some help from a teenager, and began learning a new way of making photographs. It has not been an easy process but I am finding new ways to work digitally. I continue to love the old way, though, the beautiful luster and depth of photographs printed on silver paper.

I took the Canon to Cuba on the second trip. The big lens was heavy, cumbersome, and obnoxious. I realized that I was being seen as another tourist despite not wearing Bermudas and a camera vest. I stuck out, never feeling comfortable. I examined the work closely when I got home, but only some of it passed muster. It did not show a strong personal connection with the person that I was looking for. I wanted a direct face with clear eyes. No artsy stuff with shadows or mood lighting.

In September 2011, I had a serious accident. A big mower I was riding overturned and fell on my back. I lay in bed for four months wearing a chest brace that made me look like a turtle. The spinal break was so severe I had to use a walker to get back on my feet. That accident happened five days before I had planned a 2011 visit to Cuba with permission from the U.S. government. The trip was delayed but my good surgeon helped me with a letter to the Treasury Department to get me back to Cuba in 2012.

My back continues to heal though the pain is still with me, but I can walk well enough. So I decided I'd try a different approach. I would not take the heavy Canon D5—instead, my new Apple iPhone. It came equipped with an eight megapixel camera. Why not? I could hold it in my hand. It was not showy, not like that big Canon. I'd try it and look for a good result.

I immediately saw the iPhone was the perfect camera for what I wanted to do—work with a more personal touch.

Photographers should always understand the implications of how they make photographs. I learned my method over time by listening to how I felt about what I was doing. The methods can be broken down into three ideological/political ideas: the Capitalist approach—the photograph I take is mine; the Socialist approach—I made this photograph but it is ours, implying an understanding, an agreement between the photographer and the subject; and the Humanist approach—it's ours and we always share in this photograph. That is to say, the photographer always gives something back when he or she makes a photograph. In my case, I always paid, when possible, for photographs. Making a photograph has to be fair, is my feeling.

Of course, there is one other method, the Cartier-Bresson method, that is: to steal the photograph. He famously said that all a photographer needed to make a good photograph was one eye and two good feet.

Cubans were interested in my tiny iPhone device.

"Wow! What's this you are holding, a phone, a camera too?" I was asked. That helped to set up a friendly dialogue. When I was sure that everyone was comfortable, everyone in agreement, I made photographs.

I will admit that I could not do this with several market scenes, where many people were involved. I sat quietly and waited, like Banu had told me, and occasionally I made a photograph.

The only challenge with the iPhone is keeping it steady. The hand is not a tripod. I leaned against walls, put the camera on sills, pressed it against door frames to get it steady.

I had to go back on several occasions and remake photographs that were fuzzy. Havana is not without iPhones, of course, but they are rare. I saw many tourists with the Samsung Galaxy, which makes better photographs than the iPhone.

For ten days I walked the streets of Centro Havana, an area between Havana Viejo (Old Havana) and Miramir, where wealthy Havanans live.

The appallingly filthy streets are lined with shabby classical buildings—model portraits of decrepitude. Overflowing containers spilled garbage while dogs, cats, and other living creatures poked in the mess looking for a mouthful of food. After dark one evening, I was standing near a street corner when I felt something spongy under my foot. I pressed it several times and it sprang back disconcertingly each time. Looking down, I found a plump dead mouse under my foot.

Each day from early morning to sunset, I wove through as many streets as possible. My injured back got very sore late by evening and I'd find a bar and have a beer. They were rough-looking places, but I found them friendly. I'd cautiously ease into a bar to rest and I was always waved over and usually offered a Crystal beer, a light beer similar to Coors Light.

The conversation was light too: "Where are you from? Oh! United States. I have a cousin living in New Jersey"—or Miami or North Carolina.

I didn't get into political discussions. I was told that Cubans liked Americans but were unsure if lifting the embargo would be a good thing for Cuba. I made several photographs in these bars. None turned out well. Beer drinking always morphed to rum drinking, a favorite of Cubans, and after a while, I'd leave before the drinking got too heavy.

All bars opened on Sunday morning and the men were there, some women too, drinking rum before church. What an appealing tradition! Drink enough rum and you can handle any sermon, any length.

My little iPhone never failed me even though I worried that the quality of the photographs would not be good. 'When I return to the United States,' I thought, 'I'll find a program that adds pixilation for more detail.'

Havana, like most old cities, is in a state of constant repair—partly the result of the U.S. Embargo. Garbage collection is poor. Street repair, the same. Buildings look neglected, grinders hum, jackhammers vibrate, as if the world was being built, but in this case, it seems to be trying to catch up or hang on.

Mornings are relatively calm, with people out in the street going to work, sweeping the sidewalk, an old woman lowering a basket from a second-story balcony to fetch a loaf of bread from her neighbor down below, and many others deep into the common ritual of standing in the doorway and watching the street. Cubans stand in the doorway in the morning and the evening, reminding me of growing up in my native Madison, N C, where folks sat on their porches in the evening watching the day fade.

People weave through the street each morning, most walking with plastic bags in their hands for the market. A plastic bag that we throw away, costs one Cuban peso. That is not much money for us, but it is enough so that Havanans save their plastic bags and use them again.

My first day in the street I had the feeling I was in a gigantic insect colony, a humming sound all around me. As with bees, the street activity was alive and purposeful: going to the market, going to work by moving along the narrow streets, and stopping momentarily to talk to a friend.

The old buildings where people live all have crumbling marble stairs. There must be a million steps of marble in Havana, most of it harvested from mines in western Cuba, at Minas de Matahambre, "mines of killing hunger." The steps are worn by degree and one can ascertain almost the size of a family by the wear on the steps. As I see it, Havana may have enough marble to cover the entire state of Rhode Island.

Almost all the buildings are styled like row houses in Charleston, SC. But in this case, they are built of stone and cement with rooms along a deep interior walkway used for potted plants. A living room is located in front facing the street, a kitchen and dining room are in back. Some have two stories and others even three or four, each floor with the same plan.

Dogs wander the streets unleashed in this part of the city, though I never heard a dog bark or growl at me while walking the streets. They were everywhere and they were never edgy or threatening. Never! What does this say about Cuban culture?

Back in rural North Carolina, dogs will tear you to pieces if they can get their teeth in your leg. I fought them for years, both riding a bicycle and walking. Was dog behavior one of those subtle clues that showed the true moral shape of a culture? Not much stuff to protect, so why train your dog to be mean? Everyone lives with modest means. No one has a showy house crammed full of valuables unless you are fortunate enough to live in Miramar. Maybe that is it—nothing to protect or nothing to *fear.*

I decided to follow a dog one day. See what he was up to, where he went. This particular canine was a terrier mix and he seemed to be enjoying himself in the city. He pranced, his small body shaking from side to side. I followed him for fourteen blocks as he zigged and zagged along the streets, among the passersby, making an occasional toilet stop. He had been well-trained, for afterward he always scratched the pavement with his hind legs, several times, in an attempt to cover his mess.

He went into several houses, unannounced, not ever a bark. He'd come out and on we'd go with my tiny camera hoping I could record his stroll. Finally he disappeared into a house and stayed. Was this his home? Quite possibly the home of his girlfriend and he was having his morning shag. More likely, he was onto me following him and had decided to wait me out. I left and was curious about what I would find next along the street. Crossing into the next block, I spotted a man dumping empty aluminum cans down the middle of the less traveled street Gloria. When I asked him why he was putting them in the street, he smiled and said, "You watch."

In a few minutes along came a big truck and ran right over them, then another truck, and several cars and the drivers seemed to be enjoying the sound of the cans crunching under their wheels. I was witnessing a very ingenious method of compacting. When they were thoroughly flat, he bagged the smashed cans and hauled them off.

IV.

I left Mexico for Cuba late in the afternoon. Cubans at Cancun International were lined up with toasters, televisions, computers, and even car tires, all to be checked in as baggage.

"Excuse me, please," I heard to my right and turned to see a young woman.

"Can you favor do for me––carry my bag to Havana. You are a North American? Yes!

You can take it in." She was holding a colorfully stitched bag, plump with stuff.

"I'm sorry," I said, "I cannot do it. I may get in trouble, too!"

She lowered her chin, looked at me with pleading eyes as if there was something extra in it for me. She licked her lips and smiled broadly and again said, "Please?"

"I'm sorry, but no!" I told her.

The plane landed an hour later in Havana to wild cheering and hand clapping. Anxious Cubans, not used to flying, were happy to be home, and in a real sense, they were also smart. They understood well that thousands of tons of metal can fall out of the sky easily and they were expressing honestly the good feeling everyone on board had when the plane touched down. I clapped and cheered right along with them.

I rode into the city of Havana after dark. The taxi driver was friendly, talking as we weaved in and out of heavy traffic. His arm went up with a quick motion and he pointed to a bus. Bicyclists were clinging to any part they could get a hold onto for a free ride. Traffic was speeding along at 60 kilometers, almost 38 mph, and those bikers were holding on! One hand on the bus—the other steering their bike.

We drove through dark crumbling streets alive with people walking everywhere. Walking and shouting back and forth while cars scurried through these narrow streets. I was alarmed, thinking I might have to spend the night on one of these wretched streets. The taxi driver stopped and pointed at 746 Neptuno Street. I rang the buzzer and in a minute the door flew open and there stood my host for the night, Julia, with a clear-eyed face to welcome me. We climbed two flights to a clean home and a room adequate for me. Next morning after a good night's rest, I was walking the streets of Havana relieved to see the city in daylight.

Old-world Greek and Roman architecture, open street markets, Middle Eastern flavors, and African colors with a European style dominate the city. Quite a mix. Cuba began as a staging area for the Spanish conquistadors opening up Mexico and South America. Eventually Havana became the great Spanish colonial city because of its natural harbor.

Despite the many magnificent buildings in decay and falling apart, the power of this once great city is tangible. Brimming with people walking in the streets, on the narrow sidewalks, along with cars, sidecar motorcycles whizzing by, bicycle taxis, and old, worn-out American-made cars still functioning as taxis. People are everywhere—some walking fast, others strolling, mothers with babies in their arms, men repairing their cars or motorcycles in the street, jackhammers busting up concrete, street vendors pushing small vegetable carts, green-eyed men and green-eyed women sashaying in and out of houses, their doors unlocked during the day. A deep quietness at dawn soon builds into a city hum—but by evening the humming energy turns up with force to become a symphony of shouting, shaking, and loud, reverberating music that dies away toward midnight again like a slowly cooling shooting star. Words do little justice to these sounds, this cadence, but music I could imagine. Stravinsky, Gershwin and Bizet mixed together—that would come close.

There is little to steal, so the doors are open most of the day in Centro Havana. Everyone has about the same modest stuff. There is no reason to steal, except for money. Doors fly open, people in and out, shouting cheerfully as they come. All the energy is friendly, no super beings beneath those top rhythms, as far as I can hear and sense.

Lanky black men, tall strong black men, stand around on street corners as do whites, like sentries posted for guard duty. Sometimes they talk to a passerby, sometimes the conversations get heated, arms flying and faces lighting up. But there is no sense of urgency or anger in these men. It is friendly give-and-take delivered with emotional Latino flare. They may be talking about getting a game of dominoes started. Spur-of-the-moment games pop up outdoors on sidewalks all over the city all day long.

There are many shades of black men and the same goes for whites. Black men can be tar black, dusty black, matte black, reddish black, caramel black, and tan black. Blacks understand that they are equal citizens. Whites are snow white like ghosts, a slightly toasted white, a more tan white, and an olive-skinned white. Green eyes abound. I asked one green-eyed man where those eyes came from. "Spain! Catalonia," he said, firing his eyes at me fullbore.

V

The one thing that defines Havana business besides tourism is the repair shop. Cubans don't have much stuff, but they value what they have. When something needs repairing, they take it to a service technician. At one stop I saw five such technicians seated behind a long table. At each station there was a working light and a number posted overhead. Pick a number and wait your turn.

A woman seated at a station explained her broken fan while the fixer listened and diagnosed the problem. In less than ten minutes he had it solved and sent her on her way. People were lined up with irons, computers, vacuum cleaners, radios, televisions, you name it, and it was repaired. Repair shops, I soon found, were all over the city.

Fixing things in the United States has become almost a subversive occupation. We use it, then throw it away when it is worn out or try to sell it at a yard sale. What a contrast. Fix something that is broken and fix it again. Don't throw it away. The idea of fixing things as opposed to throwing them away points up a clear difference between capitalism and communism.

The idea of planned obsolescence was a capitalist idea cooked up by a group of brilliant economists after World War II as a means of maintaining jobs. Make stuff that doesn't last and you've got yourself a secure job market. Not a bad idea at the time, and it did help to grow the job market after the war.

Most Americans don't believe they've bought junk, but when the chair starts to wobble, the toaster isn't working so well, they take it out to their yard and have themselves a big Saturday-morning yard sale, this refuse displayed all over a beautiful lawn. They hope that someone will come along and give them something for their worn-out junk. People do come and paw over the stuff and buy things, knowing they might need fixing, but they buy it with the thought in mind that they can fix it when they get home. Sometimes it does get fixed—good for another few days. Odd but true. I'm guilty myself. Most of the stuff sold in yard sales is disgusting junk, but Saturday-morning yard sales have become a new form of moveable feast and entertainment for the bored who want to unearth a treasure. It's so easy to love things, even when they're given to breaking.

The large estate sales, massive yard sales, are sad occasions. I've participated in some, looked at all the personal stuff accumulated in a lifetime out there in the yard for everyone to see and prowl around and paw through. All those saved items that represent real memories for the sellers—or for the deceased whose front yard is the locus of the sale. What does such exposure say about the loss of American personal and social graces—our sense of decency and respect, to a certain extent, is trashed when we expose to prying public eyes those items our loved ones cherished.

The endgame of the throwaway economy is the destruction of the environment. Most people understand this problem, but nothing significant is done to correct it. Rip up the trees, mine the land for all the precious minerals and metals you can get, mine it for all it's worth, suck all the oil out of the ground, pollute the atmosphere with carbon dioxide, fill the landfills with our junk. What the hell, we're on top of things! The idea of controlling growth, managing resources, is anathema to our way of thinking, despite all the lip service we pay to the problem.

Another way to look at the fix-it idea is that it creates jobs. People who fix things have jobs. Don't get me wrong. We do have people fixing things in the U.S. Plumbers, appliance repairmen, and an occasional shoe repair shop in a strip mall. It is almost impossible to find a tailor but some are creeping in with the flood of new immigrants from Asia. Nobody can fix a kitchen mixer, or an iron, or a blender, or an electric razor, though. Nor will they be able to put a soldering iron to a broken smart phone.

The smart phone brought me into an interesting conversation I'd had before I left Mexico with Ward Silver, an electrical engineer living in St. Louis. Ward may write a book that has been swirling in his mind, *The Point of Presence.* The thesis is this: The present as we know it, that which is right in front of us, is morphing into a visual abstraction—digital photographs taken on the smart phone. Ward perceives that our lives are now built around the smart phone, the new point of presence, the most entrancing locus of our attention now and the "place" where we watch/feel most alive. The smart phone image of a thing or action is the prime conferrer of authority, the reference we measure what's true and what's not.

Ward had seen a group of young people at a dance performance.

"They were not looking at the performers, they were looking at the LCD screens on their smart phones during the entire performance, making photographs," he said.

He observed that all that time, they were engaged with their phones. The phone and the photograph had become more important to them than watching the live performance, thus the point of presence had shifted down one grade from the real to the abstract via their smart phone.

Ward has a marvelous book in mind that takes a clear look at technical advances and how they are changing our world. I hope he finds enough time to write it.

So is there anything wrong with this? Indeed! I recall seeing fifty smart phones held over user's heads as they gathered around, making clicks of the Mona Lisa in Paris. Nobody seemed interested in the texture of the paint, the colors, the form, the degree of lifelike representation the painter had achieved, or the mood of the painting. They wanted to "take" a photograph away from the painting—their new presence, and record that they have been there, seen the Mona Lisa. Thus, substance in the world is no longer important, but show/representation is and the show—and the user's style—revolves around the smart phone. It is the first thing people grab in the morning or when they go to the beach. Marshall McLuhan was correct: "The medium is the message."

Economist Robert Heilbroner in *The Worldly Philosophers: Lives, Times and Ideas of Great Economic Thinkers* (Simon and Schuster, 1953) writes that capitalism will fail, destroying itself by its extreme quest for material gain. Then he went to his grave watching capitalism triumph to a degree and in ways he never expected. As I sat there looking at this repair shop operate efficiently in Havana, it occurred to me that in the long view Heilbroner might be right. And those plastic bags that you have to buy here for a peso? That's proof, plus it makes good sense!

But what is keeping the U.S. economy going today? New stuff. Fifteen flavors of water. Yes, water! Plain old water. And eight new kinds of vacuum cleaners; twelve new kinds of dog food; new soaps every week and fast-breaking new cereal types and brands. Americans are swimming in a sea of variety.

So the newness of things is what attracts the buyer today and keeps markets thriving. In fact, if people decided not to buy, our economy would implode because 70% of our economy is generated by consumer spending.

Moore's Law has also boosted our economy in ways not always clear. The law maintains that computer power will double every two years. So far it has worked as the fusion of physics and computer technology has been economically profitable. That law explains the millions of jobs and new products streaming into domestic and foreign markets. Is there an end to economic speed/fusion/profit?

"Nobody really knows," Ward Silver said, then laughed and smiled. "It could all go poof one day, David, and we'd be back to clubs and bows and arrows."

Maybe those little Indian women from Chiapas, Mexico, who sew animals from scraps of cloth and sell them along the roadside know something.

VI.

The country was in a tailspin for a time after the Russians dissolved relations with Cuba in 1991. Russian oil and fertilizer for crops were lost. Resourceful Cubans turned to organic farming as the solution. Today Organiponic gardens thrive throughout the country and in cities on small vacant plots and on rooftops there are tidy plots for growing vegetables. Cuban mastery of this gardening technique has become a model for the world.

By the sixth afternoon of inhaling exhaust fumes, I thought I should check my email. In the lobby of the Hotel Colina that was being renovated, I found an old computer. They don't tell you how to go on-line in Cuba. It is up to you and your computer skills. I needed help! That's when I met Lissa Goldstein, who was working away on another computer. We soon had my computer up. Lissa, a very accommodating 28-year-old American, works for SoleFood Street Farms, a Vancouver, British Columbia, organization that promotes urban gardening. She told me she was studying organic farming in Havana.

Her trip also had added significance. In1988, her father, Steve Goldstein, then the Moscow correspondent for the *Philadelphia Inquirer,* traveled to Cuba with Soviet Premier Mikhail Gorbachev. Gorbachev's trip was cut short because of a devastating earthquake in Armenia. He left Cuba after a parade and a brief meeting with Castro, leaving the pool of reporters stranded in Havana for a week. Lissa's father, 39 at the time, told her that on the way to Cuba, their entourage took a Russian Aeroflot plane that stopped over in Gander, Newfoundland to refuel. It turned out three of the Soviets officials defected there. The Russians went after them, tried to track them down and drag them back to the plane, but they got away.

Lissa had talked to a Cuban who witnessed the Gorbachev parade. "He probably saw my father that day," she said, pleased now as she stood on soil where her father, today a free-lance writer living in Maryland, once worked as another kind of observer.

When Lissa returned to Vancouver, she blogged her impression of Cuba under the heading, My Farming Fantasies:

> Cuba had the same golden glow that radiated from California when I was a teenager. I envisioned the pictures of Mecca with Cuba as the center and thousands of barefoot and dirty farmers in overalls facing it and bowing. That's where I was—Cuba.
>
> Two days ago I returned from my much anticipated trip to 'mecca.' The farmers I met were remarkable and charismatic, the farms beautiful. My visions of Cuba as an island utopia where all food consumed is grown next door by vegetable-worshiping people were fantastic.
>
> According to my sources (i.e. casual conversation with Cubans), they consume more rice per capita than China and almost all of it is imported. The vegetables (though organically and locally produced) are, as far as I can tell, largely a garnish or a small side dish. Sugar is king. Followed closely by pork. Spaghetti and pizza of varying degrees of artificiality have a strange hold on the nation and Cuba doesn't grow much, if any, wheat.
>
> The moral of this story is that you should always moderate your expectations. Though this reality check was somewhat disappointing at first, I still find Cuba's agriculture remarkable.

Vegetables are sold at local markets throughout Havana. A tomato I ate was so delicious that I bought a sackful, washed them up and ate them with cucumber, onion, and guava fruit. I'd never tasted a tomato like this but I'd read in *Gourmet* magazine that the best tasting tomato should have a green top. The Cuban tomato has a verdant top when picked ripe and that color shades ever so slowly into the deep red meat, lovely in its own right. It is not a hybrid. That explained its good flavor. But I couldn't find seeds to buy. I could have plucked some out of a tomato and dried them, but the thought never occurred to me then.

I needed a haircut and my host Julia told me where to go. The barber was an older man, maybe 80. When I entered his shop, he was slowly unfolding a towel that held his tools. He waved to the chair—an old wooden one. I asked him to cut just a small amount off all around. He whacked away, breathing heavily. Done cutting, he pulled out a straight razor and began to strop it on a long leather belt hanging from his chair. He could have cut my head off with that blade, it was so sharp.

Carefully he edged around my ears, his head down, eyes concentrating as he shaved down my neck on both sides. When he finished, he swiped his hand in an open tin with something that looked like Crisco, slapped his hand on my head, and began blending this stuff all through my hair. I thought it must be some kind of pig grease. Odorless, it was heavy, and proved almost impossible to wash out. I asked how much I owed, and he looked at me, hand unfolded outward and said, "Ten pesos Cubano." One U.S. dollar equals twenty-four Cubano pesos. I had just received a haircut for 40 cents. "Are you sure?" I asked him. He bent slightly and assured me that that was the cost.

Buying food with Cubano money at markets made me feel like a criminal. I'd go to the market early in the morning and buy enough fruit and vegetables for the evening meal, always for less than one dollar.

I returned to the house to see if I could get some of that grease out of my hair.

Soap would not do it. Julia smiled, "Cut like," she said.

"Yes, but not the grease job," I said in plain English, knowing she would not understand me.

That evening while I was eating a salad, bridge work broke loose from my upper jaw and fell out of my mouth. I took the three connecting teeth to a Cuban clinic next morning and was immediately taken to a room and placed in an old wooden dental chair with a scalloped porcelain work-tray by my head. A large, handsome woman came in and started mixing powder with another substance to make a glue. I looked at her strong purposeful eyes as she took the bridge, coated it with her mixture. Then with one hand behind my head and the other on the bridge, she pushed it back in place and held it there. When she was sure it would hold, she let go. I asked how much and she waved me out. No smile, all business, and no charge. I decided at that moment, when I got back to Mexico, I would find a Mexican dentist to permanently fix the bridge.

Time for me to get serious with Julia. "What would you think if President Obama lifted the Cuban Embargo?" I asked. Julia stood still for a moment, hands pulled together in thought, as if she didn't understand the question.

Then suddenly, "Venga aqui." With her finger, she motioned me over to her desk where she kept her manifest. "Look! June, July, August, September, October, November—one person stays here in my house each month."

Julia placed her index finger over her lips as a cautionary prologue: "They lift the embargo, I fill this manifest."

"Don't worry, Julia, I won't tell anyone," I told her. For my host's protection I have not used her real name or address.

I needed a real meal—a good Paladar, what Cubans call their eateries. Julia sent me to La Moraleja in Vedado, a beautiful restaurant with tables scattered under a canopy of bougainvillea in dappled light.

On the walk to the restaurant I spotted a group of women seated in rows inside an open-arched building. Each wore a metal triangle, shaped like a pyramid. They all were silent and they held their gaze as I made a photograph. A Cuban man who happened by told me the titanium pyramids were worn to help rejuvenate memory and reduce fatigue and stress.

My repast at La Moraleja was beans, rice, and a beer. As I was finishing, a woman came in and took the table next to me. She laid out several notebooks on her table, whipped out her phone, and started talking. She must be from Spain, I thought, white skin, businesslike demeanor, and she seemed a bit impatient. A Spanish princess, for sure. As I stood to leave she spoke:

"I saw you in the garden talking to those two black women at the Hotel Nacional. Where were they from?"

"One was from Gabon, the other Kenya," I said. "Very nice women and very aware of world events. They were both beautiful in an exotic way with lacquered skin."

"Please sit down a moment and have some coffee."

Where could this woman be from and what was she up to, I thought, taking a seat.

"Where are you from? You speak Spanish?" she asked.

"Some. Better with English. I'm from the United States."

"OK, we speak English."

"I'm from Argentina, but I have lived in New York. Worked for CNN as a journalist, Argentina bureau."

"I'm a journalist of sorts," I said and I told her I was in Cuba to do documentary work.

"What kind?"

"I'm working that out," I said. "Here, I'll show you a photograph."

I scrolled through my iPhone until I'd found a good, clear photograph of a Cuban woman in her home.

She looked at me seriously and said, "What are you doing in Cuba taking pictures of silly old women when the leader of FARC [Revolutionary Armed Forces of Colombia] is here in Cuba right now, this very day at the Habana Libre Hotel? As a journalist you must write about him. You know about FARC?"

"I've read about it. I know that they held an American woman captive for many years. What's her name?

"Yes, yes, I know," she said. "That stupid woman! She is in Paris now living it up! People don't understand FARC, they don't understand Hugo Chavez. They are both here right now in Havana because Cuba is the most peaceful nation in the western world. Cuba is the model for all Latin America. Chavez is here for an operation. They are cutting on him this very day."

"Look!" she said, shoving a FARC pamphlet into my hand. "Read this, go talk to Ivan Marquez. He is here in Havana right now. It is your real opportunity to do something good. This is what you need to be doing."

Her eyes burning with passion.

Marquez is provisional FARC leader since the Colombian military killed Alfonzo Cano in November 2011. FARC is an anti-imperialism, Marxist-Leninist revolutionary guerilla organization founded in 1964 in Colombia, South America. It funds itself through extortion and kidnapping.

"You know that you live in the most violent country in the world?" she asked.

"Do something about it!" she demanded, her eyes fierce.

It was obvious she was committed to the cause and I wanted to know if she had joined forces with FARC.

"Not yet, but I write about it for now," she said.

I told her my challenge was to make a document of the Cuban people in hopes that the work would tell an honest story about the Cuban people. What will folks see when they look at these photographs? Sadness, honesty, clear-eyed happy people? I wasn't sure.

"Will you be going back to the United States?" I asked her.

"No," she barked. "I did enjoy working in New York, but I never saw so many stupid people––well, maybe not all," she laughed, "and fat people too! Why do they eat so much? I never saw so many fat people in one place in all the world."

I had one more question: "What do you think of Obama?"

"He needs to be strong!" she said.

Then she looked at her watch, hurriedly wrote down her phone number, handed it to me and said, "You call me, we talk later. Bye," and out she went, her high heels clicking against the tile walkway.

I wanted to get a ticket to the ballet, but there was only opera for the next two weeks. I had been to the National Theater on a previous trip and witnessed a brilliant contemporary dance performance. In fact, I never took my eyes off the performer for almost two hours. It was that penetrating. One minute, the dancers were fish swimming, the next moment they morphed into birds flying in all directions. It was breathtaking.

Anyone visiting Havana comes to see that dancing is in the Cuban blood. Kids are swaying and moving their bodies to an internal rhythm all day in the street, at home, and when they learn to walk. During Russian occupation, all this energy got

Russian instruction and Russian discipline. The fusion turned Cuban dancers into world-class performers.

With no ballet tickets, I decided to stop on Paseo de Marti, the street of demarcation between Centro Havana and Old Havana. It runs right by the Capitol which looks much like a smaller version of the U. S. Capitol. Out in front, I noticed a man with an old box camera held together by black tape perched on a shaky wooden tripod —Eduardo.

He looked at me as I studied his camera. "Old Camera. Three hundred years old," he said. I was not going to refute his claim or give him a photography history lesson. So I smiled and he continued wiping his camera with a rag. That camera did look three hundred years old.

"This camera belonged to my grandfather and my father. We take photographs here for 60 years."

Impressed, I decided to have him make a photograph of me. I stood there in front of the Capitol in the noonday sun, maybe ten feet in front of his square black box, and Eduardo motioned me to be still.

Looking into his contraption, I watched as he slowly removed the lens cap, held it in his left hand for about six seconds, then put it back gently. In a minute, he had a wet paper negative. He wiped it and shook it in the sun until it was dry, and then placed it on a small slide-out easel in front of the lens. He adjusted the focus, made a second exposure, and announced, "Now positive." Three minutes later, I had a faultless, clear black and white photograph of me standing there.

The paper negative camera dates back to the 1850s. Eduardo's camera was truly an antique. Paper negative cameras were on their way out in 1912 when Graflex introduced the Speed Graphic film-holder camera. The bulky Speed Graphic was used by newspaper and magazine photographers until overtaken by the 35mm revolution in the late 1940s. New and faster films made the 35mm camera light and agile. By 1990 digital cameras began to smother the camera market and today these cameras are produced in mind boggling variety.

I decided not to ruin Eduardo's day by pulling out my iPhone and make an instant photograph.

Up the street, I spotted a group of Germans headed my way. They were tall and very pale and, thank goodness, not wearing lederhosen. The tallest of the group suddenly stopped, clutched his hands to his hips, with his elbows winged out, and began studying a piece of real estate on the corner. Like many Germans, he had an acquisitive, authoritarian demeanor. *He must be thinking like a serious German,* I said to myself, *Poland today, France tomorrow, and Cuba next week.*

He turned a knowing glance on one of his fellow travelers and nodded.

'"Here, here, Herr Obergruppenführer, we must get on this right away. The Chancellor must know immediately. Pünktlich! I want this place,"' I read his meaning.

So tall and gangly they were there, standing out like white Watusis. What were these perfectionists, these masters of punctuality doing rambling amongst a group of people who couldn't care less about time or efficiency?

I needed to get away from tourists. But before I left that street, I stopped at a French bakery, catching a smile from a good-looking young woman as I entered. She curled her index finger for me to come over.

I was polite but hungry. I told her I would stop back after I'd eaten. Still sitting outside the bakery rolling those green eyes when I came out, she dragged a chair up and motioned for me to sit. I sat down and noticed her beautiful tan skin. Her lips were painted a bright red, she had a clean, toothy smile, and her fingernails were long glue-ons.

"You looking for amor?" she said very pointedly.

"What kind of love?"

"You know, sex!"

"No, no. I'm too old for that. Look at my white hair!"

I thought that had ended it, but she insisted and tore out a scrap of paper from my notebook and wrote down her phone number.

"Here, call me later," she said, still hoping.

"No," I said. "I'm 75 years old and past all that." I thought I had shocked her into retreat, but she looked at me, smiled broadly and said, "Seventy-five is nothing! Last week I had a Canadian man. He was 84 and he was good to go."

I had to laugh. Those wily Canadians. I took the phone number, tucked it in my shirt pocket, and left. A short way down the street I looked back. She was still gazing at me, tapping her fingers on the tabletop, still wearing a yearning look in her eye.

Back across the demarcation into real-world Havana, I began seeing small window shops that I hadn't noticed before. Suddenly, they were everywhere. An open window store. Place a piece of plywood on a window sill, drape it with cloth, put some lipstick, fingernail files, pencils, notebook paper and anything else you can sell, and you have a window store. The world's smallest mini-market. One in almost every block, but you had to pay attention or you might walk right past.

Havana has no outdoor advertising. The local paper, *Granma,* does carry political ads. A full-page ad on the back page of today's paper features a large open palm, fingers down, that hangs from the top of the page. "Obama" is printed across the palm. Beneath it is the phrase: "Give me Five!" The slogan is part of a campaign for the release of the so-called Cuban Five: Gerardo, Ramon, Antonio, Fernando, and Rene, the Cuban agents convicted of spying on U.S. government facilities in 1996.

Walking down Concordia Street, I ran across a man carrying a device about the size of a chainsaw.

"What is this you have?" I asked.

"We call them bazocas here in Havana," he said and he took my pencil and spelled BAZOCAS. Mix some gasoline and old oil, start it, and it produces an oily fog that kills mosquitoes.

"Can you crank it up?"

"Yes, of course," he said in such an obliging manner. He started it and I made a photograph.

He had a schedule with addresses of homes that needed fumigating, working his way up Concordia. I watched for a while. He'd enter a home, while the residents piled out into the street and then the oily fog would start streaming out the windows and doors.

I went back to the Hotel Nacional to exchange pesos to CuCs (Cuban Convertible Pesos). A pale man with lightly freckled skin was in line in front of me. He wore a straw hat and seemed a bit impatient.

"Where you from?" I asked.

"England, the Midlands near Shropshire, and where are you from?" he asked. "You have such a strange accent."

I anticipated getting an al fresco lesson in English grammar. Offended British ears always stand ready to correct. I changed the subject with a question.

"Tell me, what is the most unusual thing you have ever seen in your life?"

"Well, yes, actually I can tell you that right off. The breathtaking desert scapes in Jordan late in the evening. I've never seen anything like it since. That desert is where they filmed *Lawrence of Arabia.*"

He gave me a hard look. Hmm. He was still thinking about my speech and accent. Leaning forward from his six-foot frame, he looked directly into my eyes and said, "It's elocution, my boy, elocution."

At least I had known it was coming. I controlled myself and walked away thinking how much I wanted to smash my fist through the crown of the silly straw hat he was wearing.

Back on the street, a black woman came alongside me and asked where I was from. I told her North Carolina and she beamed, "Oh, I have a friend from Raleigh, North Carolina. He comes here to Cuba. He once took me on a trip all over Cuba. It was my first time to see my country. At first, I thought you were from Italy." She beamed again. Distant friends, made on the spot—made accidentally through a sort of geographical proxy. "Well," she said, "enjoy Cuba!" and she moved on.

I had many similar chance meetings in Havana. Nobody pushing or hustling, just a recognition and connection with no hidden agenda. Much friendly, welcoming talk. The Cubans certainly understand that as a people they are all in this world together.

I crossed over onto San Rafael Street where boys played baseball with sticks and bottle caps. I watched them for quite a while. Swinging a little skinny stick at a bottle cap is what has trained so many great hitters from Cuba.

They were likely unaware that by swinging a stick at a bottle cap they had created a perfect model for training to be a great hitter. Batting cages good, sticks and bottle caps, better.

Time in the streets was closing in on me fast. I'd been walking for seven days, just looking and soaking it all up. I got to thinking about a cool drink and headed back to Marti, finding an Italian restaurant. When I walked in, I saw a young woman talking to an older man. *Father and daughter? Maybe.*

But she was dark and exotic and very beautiful, and he was blond, craggy, with hair on his face. 'Can't be her dad.' Almost immediately, he waved me over.

"Come have a drink with us and talk. Don't you love this place?" he said with a distinct Scandinavian accent.

"Sweden," I said.

"Yah, yah," smiling, "I'm Sven and this is Nilufer."

"And where are you from?" said the woman in perfect English.

I told her I lived in the woods in a remote central North Carolina county and I asked her the same question. She leaned forward slightly, eyes directed at me. "Istanbul."

I had never met anyone from Turkey. I was astounded by her beauty. A serenely intelligent aura radiated from her face—a placid beauty that had been made by the union of Europeans and Asians.

"I'm traveling," she said. "Europe first, Cuba, and then South America."

"Tell me about Istanbul," I said.

"Well, it is a great city, you know, and it is the only place in the world where you can swim from Asia to Europe or the reverse. Swim the Bosporus."

"Have you done it?"

"No," she said. "But each year, they have a day when you can do it if you like."

John Galt, in *The Life of Lord Byron* (ebook #10421, 2003, Chapter 23) wrote an account of Byron's travels through Asia Minor in the late 1820s and the trip to the Bosporus that inspired him to write a poem:

> The wind swept down the Euxine, and the wave
> Broke foaming o'er the blue Symplegades.

'Tis a grand sight, from off the giant's grave,
To watch the progress of those rolling seas
Between the Bosporus, as they lash and lave
Europe and Asia, you being quite at ease.

Nilufer traveled alone. I met many young women traveling solo in Havana. Getting educated, they told me, and were unafraid.

"No, not afraid," she assured me.

I had begun to feel comfortable in the streets, even after dark. Conversations with travelers always concluded with something like, "These Cubans are such friendly, sweet people. Safety must be contagious."

From my experience, I could not disagree.

Cuban manners always suggested openness and engagement. Cubans have no guns in their homes. You can't have a gun, in fact, the result of a law put in force shortly after the revolution by Castro, who clearly understood the realities of revolution and counterrevolution. The same day I talked with Nilufer and Sven, I heard people in the street talking about a mass killing in the United States. They seemed as shocked as I was. Twenty children murdered by another crazy young man with an assault rifle.

My final night in Havana, I went up to the well-known Paladar San Christobal on San Rafael Street and just happened to run into a filmmaking crew from New York working there.

I watched until they were done and made small talk with one of their helpers, Carlos, a Cuban. He asked me where I was from. I gave him the usual, and he then looked at me intensely and said, "My friend,...you be careful." I assured him I was careful and I told him how I had worked the streets day and night. He looked hard at me and said, "I don't want to spoil your dream, but you need to understand one thing. Most of these people make $15 a month working for the government, enough to just get by with food. Now Christmas is almost here and they can't buy anything and they might need a little money." Carlos had my complete attention.

"They won't kill you for money," he said. "They will hit you over the head with a stick, worse, a hammer; take your wallet; and leave you in the street squirming like a big rat."

VII.

Back in Mexico, I took the 2:00 p.m. ferry to Isla Mujeres to rest up. After my tooth problem in Cuba, I found a Mexican dental clinic in Cancun and made an appointment.

Several days later, I took the ferry back to Cancun for a late afternoon dental consultation. No seats were available downstairs. I had noticed a middle-aged preppy-looking woman and I climbed the stairs to an open deck behind her. As it happened, there were so many people and so few seats I found a seat beside her. She was quite striking in profile. I always wonder about the head-turn. What will I see? This time it was a very sad face with good hair. Her hair was pulled back tight into a pony tail that fluffed open with streaks of silver. She wore white pants and a white top which set off her tan.

I didn't want this woman to think I was being forward or flirting with her. Most people who travel share a common understanding that if they tell their travel experiences to strangers they meet, they will hear a good story in return.

She was distant, not wanting to talk. She intentionally pulled her body in as I admired her beautifully tanned hands resting on her thighs.

I decided I'd ask her where she was going. She didn't respond. I'm sure she heard me, but I have a soft voice and the ferry engine was making noise. So a little louder, "Where are you going?"

She turned her head slightly. Her face was Scandinavian. Broad forehead, blue eyes.

"Florida!"

"What part?"

I could see that her lips had been chapped by too much sun. But she warmed a bit.

"I'm going back to St Pete."

"I'm going to have tooth work done in Cancun. Implants," I said.

"Well, I hear the dentists here are very good. But I'm going home. My friends thought I should come here to Isla to help with my depression."

"But doesn't Florida have enough sun?"

"Yes it does, but I needed to get away. My husband died two months ago."

"I'm so sorry," I told her and thought I should stop talking and let her have peace in her loss. But I couldn't resist knowing. He must have been less than forty years old, I figured. Much too young to die.

"How did he die?"

"He committed suicide," she said. "Killed himself with a pistol."

If that were true, where were the usual signs of the puffy-eyed widow?

As the ferry approached the port, people began to stir and I noticed my companion reach into her purse and pull out a diamond ring. This was no ordinary diamond ring. And she had no accompanying gold band.

"Wow!" I said. "That ring hocked at a pawn shop should keep you living in high style for several years."

"I just put it on so that I won't lose it," she said.

She disembarked ahead of me. As I waited on the jammed-up passageway, I saw her walk briskly down the dock. To my surprise a handsome man stood waiting there for her. She caressed him and gave him more than a peck on the cheek. After a passionate kiss, he took her arm and they left.

What a strange story hers was––the suicide, the ring, and the kiss. I wondered what was going on? All sorts of ideas ran through my mind: Could that man have been her boyfriend? Maybe even her husband? The ring alone without a gold band suggested an engagement. A diamond without a gold band might also suggest she was married, but had misplaced the gold band. Was there one clue to this riddle? Had she played a joke on me, making me feel sorry for her and thus be silent out of respect? Then I remembered, her left hand there on her thigh. No white shadow—nothing but solid tan, indicating that she was not wearing the ring on Isla Mujeres. Maybe she was having a fling on the island and she needed to get that ring back on her finger before her husband saw her without it. Was he smart enough to catch this little detail of the smooth tan? Again, this man could have been her brother, coming to take her to the airport. But a kiss like that between a brother and sister? —not likely.

I found a shady spot and waited for my driver to take me to the dental clinic.

A slight man with a bag of medicine plopped down across from me and said, "I hope you don't mind me sitting here?" His arms were red from what appeared to be burns.

He looked at me with a bit of distress in his eyes and said he had just been released from the hospital after a week fighting Dengue fever.

"Mean stuff," he said. "I live over on Isla on a boat."

His arms were covered with red splotches that he rubbed constantly with his hands. He talked a bit about how good they had been to him at the hospital. The doctors, too.

"They spend an hour with you here in Mexico, in the States four minutes while they look at their watch," he said.

"Tell me about Dengue fever."

"Well, they call it break-bone fever down here. Your muscles pull up so tight it feels like they will break your bones. Got it from one of those little brown mosquitoes. It is the female that carries it. I've been on my boat for seven years and I anchored it in that cove over there filled with mosquitoes. Bad spot."

"Where you from?" he said, changing the subject.

"A little town in North Carolina, Madison. I live out in the country. Very quiet."

"I came from San Francisco. Born there, raised a family. Was a Navy corpsman for six years, so I know about medicine."

As he was talking, an attractive Mexican woman no more than thirty-five walked over to him.

"She is my wife," he said. "Wonderful cook. Looks after me."

I was curious about this arrangement. He was at least 78 and she less than 40.

"Where did you meet your wife?"

"Mexico City. She's been with me for two years. Great companion."

As I looked at the two of them, I thought that this could be the ultimate mobile nursing-home arrangement—a beautiful Mexican woman to travel, cook, and see to your needs. She obviously cared for him. She put her hand on his frail shoulder and rubbed it as he looked fondly at her.

"I lived in the States," he continued, "but the place has gone to hell. Lots of stupid people, country is in massive debt. Hell, here in Mexico the government has no debt right now and this country is growing. You have public health or private if you like. People can get a job. They don't make much, but they make enough to live. Lose your job in the States and you wind up on the street. Americans have lost their sense of the importance of a job—the purpose of living—to work."

I regarded him and that beautiful young wife and recalled an Indian proverb: "As you are, I was; as I am, you will be." Would she stay with him?

Though agreeing with some of what he'd said, I am far from anti-American. I still love my country despite its many faults: stupid politicians, needy cult figures, fat people, and all. However, it is true that in Mexico I was getting professional dental work for eighty percent less than in the United States. The Mexicans are very good with their hands. My partner, Karen, has Chinese friends who take their vacations in Taiwan to have their teeth fixed. I probably would not have used a Mexican dentist had the price not been so exorbitant at home. Appalling what a dentist charges for one implant—upwards of $4,000 for a procedure that takes less than an hour and uses one screw.

I still have faith in our dentists, however. They've finally started holding free dental clinics for struggling Americans in North Carolina and other states. Dentists have quit going off to third-world countries to fix teeth for free, while in their own backyard charging exorbitant prices for poor and middle-class Americans.

At the dental clinic, a dental surgeon and three assistants were waiting for me. All were wearing face masks, surgical caps, rubber gloves, and clean, starched blue uniforms. They went right to work, no chattering, and in less than an hour two implant screws had been torqued into my upper jaw. The surgeon told me to stand and drop my pants, and he gave me an injection. "That is for pain, David." Good for a laugh from the staff.

As I was leaving, a Seattle woman came in for dental work. She told me implants there started at $5,000 apiece. Dentists, she said, had become loan sharks. "They loan you the money to fix your teeth and you pay it off in installments at a high interest rate."

After dark I boarded the ferry back to Isla Mujeres. I climbed to the open upper deck, found a seat, and as the boat slipped across the channel I tipped my head as far back as I could so that I was looking at night blackness filled with millions of bright stars. I felt like a space traveler, the hum of the boat's engine my rocket-powered space vehicle.

I met a couple from California back in Isla the same evening. Dan Nelson and his wife, though I don't remember her name. The subject worked its way to health care in the United States since I told them about getting excellent dental work in Mexico. Dan's wife had been a nurse and she had that look of "I've seen it all."

"I can tell you one thing," she said, exploding the myth that full insurance is your safety net in the United States.

"You can have all the insurance in the world, but if you have an accident, get seriously ill, or have an attack on a weekend or holiday or any day really, all that money you spent on insurance is not going to do you a bit of good unless a good team of doctors or surgeons, and nurses, are on duty when you come in."

VIII.

In the Comida Economio on Avenue Juarez in Isla, I was resting and working over my notes when three young Americans came in. They had just returned from Cuba and they were excited about the experience. I asked if I could join them. I wanted to know what they saw, how they felt. I've chosen not to use their names.

The three-week trip turned them inside out, they all agreed. They were having a bit of a problem getting turned inside out again adjusting to the consumer world. They were stunned by the real-world feel of Cuba to the point that it was surreal to them. Hardly any native Cubans texting, nobody standing around with a cell phone to their ear, no billboards, no television advertising, no grocery specials fliers, just plain people walking and talking in the streets and in restaurants.

These twenty-year-olds were a bit shocked to see that life goes right on just fine without the constant barrage of advertising pushing you to buy something.

"Most of the stuff we buy, we really don't need," one of the young men said. "You know all that advertising in the U. S., it really is a lie—so exaggerated and dishonest. The stuff you buy is never really the same. It is like a bait and switch game. They dangle the carrot, you bite but you don't really get what you bargained for. Maybe occasionally.

"In Cuba nobody is pushing things. Everything is real. Stuff is there but it isn't being pushed on you. If a person really needs something, they'll get it from a neighbor or friend or they will go find what they want and negotiate a price."

They'd stayed in homes of professional families during their three-week jaunt. They'd learned from political discussions with their hosts. Their conclusions boiled down to this: Both capitalism and communism have their good and bad points. All three said Cubans appeared satisfied with the present system. Their hosts were educated people, though, and those sentiments might not be true throughout Cuba.

One went so far as to say he thought Cuba was more democratic than the United States. His observation was based on the fact that the Communist Party does not run the country—members of Council of State do most of the decision making. Castro doesn't decide everything.

"In the provinces, people pick a slate of the smartest people to run for an office and they vote on the one they think will do the best job. No big ad campaigns—no money involved. Candidates meet with people and discuss the issues. Then they vote," he said.

One thing really stood out for all three: they never heard one bit of whining. They never saw a curled lip of scorn or dissatisfaction. Clearly these young people had seen a different political and cultural model, and I heard that they understood well that something was wrong in the United States. Some part was missing that could get

America back on a more human track. They had taken a high-quality recorder with them to pick up street sounds and, with their photographs, planned to make an art presentation combining the two.

During my ten-day trip to Havana, I never heard one negative remark about the United States. Many people told me they had family living in different parts of America. They would like for it to be easier to travel back and forth, but they were not interested in leaving Cuba. Only the younger people who had tasted the material temptations via Miami television or those whose families had been split by emigration were eager to leave.

Had Mitt Romney taken a stroll through Cuba, he'd probably have said, "Hell fire, one hundred percent of these people are slackers!"

The story that percolates through our country is this: Cubans are all building boats, secretly waiting for the right moment to leave.

I heard Cubans say they had reservations about lifting the U. S. Embargo. They fear the big money will come in, take over, and they will again be under the thumb of capitalism or some form of economic imperialism as in the days of dictator Fulgenico Batista who ruled the island until Castro's takeover in January, 1959.

IX.

At the airport in Cancun, on January 6, 2013, I found my gate and a comfortable seat. I'd about given up on finding a really good story, but I still had two hours to kill. Fairly soon, people started streaming in and a small Mayan man happened to sit down beside me. He had those large trusting eyes, that seem to float on the small head that was as round as a volleyball. *Pure Mayan* I thought. *Must be.*

He made himself comfortable and placed two small bags on the floor just in front of him, then twisted his body in my direction and said,

"Ver es jou going?"

"I'm headed back to the United States."

He smiled broadly and said," I like ah gringos. I haddah gringo amigo en Houston, viery reech!"

"It is good to have rich friends," I said.

"Yes," he said thoughtfully, and he smiled slowly and broadly and he seemed to be contemplating something.

"Jou wanna ear a goot estorie, my friend?"

I was all ears. "Yes, of course. Please, I will listen." I have transcribed his broken English for clarity.

"Well, this rich friend he live in Texas, Houston. I don't know his work, but he has a lot of money. Maybe doctor, lawyer, businessman...

"I met him here in the airport just like you and me now. Almost the same gate. I was flying to San Cristobal de las Casas, to visit my daughter, he was flying to Houston.

"This man he was smart. Spoke perfect Spanish, even a bit of Nauthula dialect. Well, he told me he needed some help.

"What kind of help?"

"I need someone to build a dance floor down in the jungle. Very remote place, can you help?"

"He didn't even know I was a builder, it just happened that way, So I said, of course, of course! He wanted the floor made of wood large enough so that fifty people could dance on it.

"Yes, yes, I can do it, I told him. I'll need some help and some money, of course.

"No problem, he said, and he pulled out a little envelope and counted out $7,000 U.S. dollars. He had a map and he showed me approximate location where he wanted the floor. It was down along Rio Usumacinta in a remote part of the jungle. Nobody lives close by. I knew the area. Maybe a few Indians living there in the jungle.

"Then he said he wanted the floor built first, then a shelter with mosquito netting beside the dance floor. Yes, I said, I can do that. This was in September, 2012."

"You will do the work!" He smiled. Happy man.

"Of course, I have friends. They will help me.

"The last thing he said before he left that day was this: The night of December 31, I want an open wooden boat large enough for fifty people docked in the river at Emilio Zapata, a small town in the jungle.

"I gave him assurances, my phone number and address where I live at Puerto Morelos, and I told him that I could take care of everything. Mayans are very resourceful, you know.

"I got to work. I found that place on the map. It was some distance from the Belize /Mexican border out in the middle of nowhere. There are lots of big Banyon trees with flared roots that look like elephant ears, and long dark roots hanging from the limbs like witches' hair.

"Thick undergrowth. It took a few days to clear out a spot. I floated the lumber down the river. No other way to get it there. Soon we had the floor built just off the ground about a foot. I decided to make the shelter from poles in the jungle and cover it with palm leaves. Keep down cost.

"He'd call occasionally and say, How is it coming? I'd tell him, It's coming, and he seemed satisfied. Nice man. And then he called back that same day with an afterthought.

"Can you get me a generator and a sound system?"

"Easy, I told him. He sent more money."

"A month before December 31, he called again and asked me to find twenty beautiful Indian women and twenty large ostrich feathers. Dye those feathers purple. Have the women and the feathers ready at the boat. I just happened to know a man who raised ostriches for eggs and meat and I knew I could get the feathers. Everything is coming along.

"I did not hear from him until a week before we were supposed to take him down the river. He wanted me to be sure to get torch lamps and Bob Marley music.

"It is done, I told him

"Oh, and one more thing, he said. Find a five gallon container, fill it with gasoline, and put it on the boat. Be at the boat at 8:00 p.m. ready to go.

"Well, everything was ready, the boat, the women—had them dressed in colorful clothes, the feathers, the torches, and we waited.

"Just at the point of 8:00 p.m. December 31, like he said, a bus pulled up and unloaded fifty women and men, all well-dressed people. And the Gringo all by himself, except he had this young Mayan boy no older than 16 years old carrying a saxophone.

"They boarded in darkness and we began to drift down the river, no engine, just the boat riding the current slowly, the moon already up glittering on the rippling water. The dark jungle wet and breathing warm moist air.

"For a very long time it was quiet. Totally quiet. The people were not afraid, they were absorbed by the unusual sounds of the jungle, the roosting birds talking to each other just before bedtime, the light breeze rustling through the palm leaves, the sound of water. It was very beautiful.

"Then the Gringo signaled the boy with the saxophone and he walked to the front of the boat, and started playing this song, 'When A Man Loves A Woman.'

"Well, my friend, I never heard such beautiful music. The boy closed his eyes, leaned his head back and played that music with all his heart, played it like he was playing to one of the Mayan deities out in the cosmos. When he finished, the crowd was so stunned, they couldn't clap or shout—that would have destroyed the beauty of what they had heard.

"After a bit, the Gringo started passing out drinks. All kind of drinks, wine, beer, whiskey, mescal. What ever you want and the crowd started to warm up.

"Those women I had dressed so well used the ostrich feather to brush the mosquitoes away and to keep the air moving among these people. An unusual sight it was, I tell you. Those feathers waving back and forth, the drinking and laughing all now breaking the peaceful atmosphere of the jungle.

"I had prepared a dock for landing, and after a two-hour drift, we arrived at this place in the jungle and everybody got off. I put the fire to the torches, turned the music on as I had been instructed, and they began to dance and drink.

"They danced and they danced and they didn't stop—on into the night until daybreak of the new year. They mostly passed out from exhaustion and drinking and were scattered around on the ground like corpses.

It looked like the Jonestown suicide massacre, them all lying there.

"But the Gringo was still standing. I watched him walk among the bodies and then sit down on the edge of the dance floor with a distant look in his eye and a light smile on his face. *Wonder what he's thinking*? I thought at the time.

"At 9:00 a.m. sharp, he stood up, started poking his guests with a stick, 'Come on, time to go, come on,' he was saying and they began to get up and he told them–—'Time to leave.'

"Then, he said to me, 'Get the gasoline, pour it on the floor, and the shelter. When I'd finished, he pulled out a match, lit one of the torches, and threw it on the dance floor. The place exploded like, what you say—napalm?

"His friends were standing along the riverbank shielding their faces from the heat. Then one by one they began to clap and cheer.

"When the fire had died down, he gave the order to load the boat, we headed up-river, they piled in the bus, and left. I've not heard from him since. Oh, and he was a very small man. He had a sharp nose and he looked like a little bird."

"That is an unbelievable story," I said.

" Jes, jes, I know," he said. "As God es my weetness, it is true."

AFTERWORD

January 14, 2013, the Cuban government announced that its citizens would no longer be required to obtain an exit permit before leaving the country. There had been mounting pressure by Cubans to drop the hated permit process which usually took years.

Now Cubans are able to travel abroad with their passport and a national identification card. Cubans can be away from their country for up to two years without threat of losing their property.

This easing was a welcome announcement to Cubans, who were usually treated as traitors when they applied for permits. President Raoul Castro, who took over from his ailing brother Fidel in 2008, has gradually eased restrictions in many areas of politics and business. Cubans still face the daunting process of obtaining a passport—a process that could be as exasperating as getting an exit permit.

This latest reform came on the fiftieth anniversary of the Cuban missile crisis, the closest the world has ever come to a nuclear war, as the United States and Russia squared off over Soviet missiles placed on the island just 90 miles off the U. S. coast.

It is obvious to any visitor that Cubans are poor materially. Compare what they have or don't have to what we have in the United States and you see a tremendous distortion. Yet, I found the folks strong of spirit and character.

Cubans, who grew to maturity without having the temptation of a Wal-Mart, or a Costco or a huge mall don't feel cheated. I didn't hear any grumbling. They do want basic necessities: a good toaster, a computer, a better washing machine, or a better automobile, but they have not been subsumed by materialism. Still there are Cubans who want to leave for different reasons. In early April this year, seven members of the National Ballet of Cuba defected while on tour in Mexico. They wanted more artistic freedom.

Cubans have lived without taxation for fifty years, but that may be changing. Most government revenue today comes from state run companies [90%] and the government allocates these resources to fund free social services. All Cubans receive some sort of government assistance—however meager it might be.

In January 2013, the government began a taxation program as an add-on along with easing restrictions on free enterprise. Cubans, you can be sure, will be screaming about taxes, but it can only help. Maybe there will now be enough money in the coffers to get the garbage off the streets of Havana.

Those ten days walking the streets from daylight to sundown, I never saw a beggar. Beggars don't exist because families and neighbors don't allow this to happen nor does the government. While beggars are not evident, street hustlers are common—people who are trying to wrest extra money to supplement their poor government salaries. So Cuba is poor but it is not dystopian. The economic void has been filled with an energetic arts movement, advances in organic agriculture, and a strong emphasis on education and public health. School dropouts rarely exist in Cuba which has the highest literacy rate [95%] in the western hemisphere. Medical and dental care are free. The doctor to patient ratio is one of the highest in the world. The government maintains over 400 clinics and 267 hospital throughout the country.

I did ask several people if they ever felt the urge to leave Cuba. Truth is, most of the Cubans don't want to see the United States embargo lifted and they do not want to leave. They fear a corporate take over worse than the days of Batista. As to leaving their homeland, I got a resounding no. "Why would we want to leave Cuba. This is our home," I heard.

A few weeks after I left, the French daredevil, Alain Robert, 'Spiderman' scaled the 27 story hotel Habana Libre without safety equipment while a huge crowd cheered him on. I'm sorry I missed that event.

Working on this book, I did slow myself down. I saw more of what real Cuba is like. Watching impromptu domino games spring up on the streets and sidewalks during working hours, I found calming and I imagined the impossibility of such a scenario in the U.S.

Most portraits in this book, as I stated earlier, were made with my iPhone camera. Using this tiny camera I was better able to establish a connection with my subjects. I never felt more comfortable making photographs as I sought close-in faces that would tell a story to the eye.

David M. Spear
May 1, 2013
Madison, North Carolina